Suicidal Thoughts

How To Deal With And Overcome Suicidal Tendencies And Feelings

By D.C. Johnson

Table of Contents

Introduction

Before you even start reading this book if you are having suicidal thoughts dial the following number: 855-478-3006. It is a suicide prevention helpline and they are available 24 hours a day 7 days a week.

According to the World Health Organization, an estimated one million people worldwide commit suicide every year. This is the equivalent of 3000 deaths per day or one life lost every 40 seconds. For each person who is successful at taking their own life there are at least 20 people who make an attempt. The global mortality rate for suicide is 16 per every 100,000 people.

Dr. Lanny Berman the President of the International Association for Suicide Prevention believes that there is a reduction in suicide when leaders make its prevention a main priority. In Australia, the restructuring of firearm legislation coincided with an increased reduction in the number of firearm related suicides. In the United Kingdom restricting the amount of over the counter medicine purchased resulted in the decrease of deaths related to intentional overdose.

It is clear from the above examples that when cultural elements are taken into consideration great strides are made in advancing suicide prevention.

The tenth leading cause of death worldwide is suicide. In America for every homicide there are two suicides. The suicide rate has increased by 60% in the last fifty years, more so in industrialized nations. Approximately 60% of all suicides happen in Asia and 16.5% of suicides in the United States are alcohol related. In comparison to the rest of the population an alcoholic has a higher risk of committing suicide. This is also true of people who abuse drugs. An estimated 33% of all suicides of people younger than the age of 35 have been diagnosed with drug or alcohol addiction.

In Western countries women attempt suicide more than men but the majority of all suicides are committed by men. In the majority of countries worldwide an estimated two-thirds of suicides among females are due to a drug overdose.

An estimated 30% of teenagers globally have had suicidal thoughts, 18% have self-harmed and 4% have attempted suicide. Out of these findings it was discovered that teenagers who identify as belonging to the punk, emo or goth culture are more like to self harm and approximately 1 in 5 have attempted suicide.

It is clear from these statistics that suicide is a major problem worldwide. If you suffer from suicidal thoughts or you know someone who does this book will provide you with methods and strategies to help you deal with suicidal thoughts.

Chapter 1: Understanding Suicide

Suicidal thoughts are also referred to as suicidal ideation and they are thoughts about how a person can carry out the act of suicide. These thoughts can range from a fleeting thought to a detailed plan.

The majority of people who suffer from suicidal ideation do not end up killing themselves, some may make an attempt and some make a deliberate plan to fail and be discovered; while others might make a careful plan to succeed.

According to research conducted in Finland, more than one fifth of people who were successful in taking their life discussed their plans with a health care professional during their last appointment before carrying out the act.

Facts About Suicidal Thoughts

- The majority of people who think about suicide don't end up killing themselves

- There are approximately 30,000 suicides in America each year.

- An estimated 4 in 5 victims of suicide in America are male.

- The majority of people who kill themselves suffer from a mental illness.

- Causes of suicidal ideation include substance abuse, anorexia, and depression.

- People who have a family history of mental illness are at risk of having suicidal thoughts.

- People who own a firearm are more likely act on their thoughts of suicide.

- There are twice as many suicides than homicides in America.

- It is possible to prevent suicidal thoughts; there is plenty of help available.

Suicide Statistics

According to the Food and Drug Administration, approximately 30,000 people commit suicide in America every year. The majority of suicides are committed by men at a rate of 80%. Among 15 to 24 year olds, suicide is the third leading cause of death. Twenty percent of people who commit suicide are in this age group.

According to the National Health Service (NHS), suicide rates in the United Kingdom have decreased in the past 20 years. Approximately 140,000 people end up in hospital each year in

England and Wales as a result of a suicide attempt. Three quarters of suicides in the United Kingdom are committed by men; the risk is highest among people between the ages of 25 to 34 years old. Suicide is the second highest cause of death among males between the ages of 15 to 44.

The NHS also states that the majority of suicides are committed by people who suffer from a mental illness such as depression. An estimated 10 to 15 percent of patients who suffer from bipolar disorder die from suicide. Approximately 4 percent of people who suffer from schizophrenia die as a result of suicide.

If you are feeling like taking your own life, these feelings may confuse or scare you. However, many people think about committing suicide some time during their lifetime so you are not alone.

There is no definitive checklist for suicidal feelings; each person will have their own unique experience. You may feel as if you are unable to cope with difficult life circumstances. The feeling that you are experiencing might not be that you want to die but that you can't continue living in your present situation.

These feelings can intensify over time, or they may fluctuate. It's common to have a limited understanding of your feelings. When you are feeling suicidal here are some feelings and thoughts that you might go through.

- Hopeless, as if living life no longer has any meaning

- Overwhelmed and tearful because of continuous negative thinking

- You are unable to see any light at the end of the tunnel

- Useless, unneeded or unwanted by others

- Desperate, as if you don't have any other choice

- As if the world would be a better place without you

- You are unable to feel anything physically

When you are feeling suicidal you may go through the following:

- A lack of sleep and waking up early

- Weight loss or weight gain because of a change in appetite

- Neglecting the way you look because you don't have the desire to take care of yourself

- Withdrawal from others

- The desire to harm yourself

- Low self-esteem and self-loathing

People experience overwhelming feelings when they are suicidal. It is difficult to state how long these feelings last because everyone is different. It's normal to feel as if you will never be hopeful or happy again. However, with the right support the majority of people who have contemplated suicide go on to live a normal and fulfilling life. Suicidal thoughts are not permanent, things will improve and you will get the motivation you need to continue living.

The faster you make someone aware of how you feel, the quicker you will be able to get the support you need to overcome suicidal feelings. However, transparency can be hard when you don't know who to trust. You may want others to understand how you feel but you are scared because:

- You don't know who to tell

- You are scared that they won't understand

- You are scared of being judged

- You are afraid that you will upset them

These thoughts and feelings are perfectly normal; however, it is important to remember that you deserve to get help and if you can reach out to the right person you will get the support that you need.

Why Am I Feeling Suicidal

Regardless of background, gender or age, anyone can experience suicidal feelings. If you have got to the point where you feel like taking your own life it is possible that you have been feeling a growing sense of worthlessness and helplessness for some time. You may not understand what has caused you to feel this way but it is generally a combination of factors. You might be experiencing some difficulties in your life that you are struggling to cope with. When you feel as if a problem is too big for you to handle it can cause you to think that suicide is the only way out. Such difficulties include:

- Physical or sexual abuse

- Doubts about your gender or sexual identity

- Religious or cultural pressure such as arranged marriage

- Postnatal depression, childbirth or pregnancy

- The death of a loved one

- Feeling like a failure or that you are inadequate

- Being incarcerated

- Loneliness or isolation

- Homelessness or money problems

- Redundancy or retirement and trying to adjust to the change

- Long-term illness or physical pain

- The end of a romantic relationship

- Domestic abuse

- Discrimination or bullying

- Mental health problems

If you don't understand why you are feeling suicidal, you might find it even more difficult to believe that there is a solution. Whatever your reason is for wanting to end your life, there is support and help available to help you to overcome and cope with these feelings.

Is My Medication Causing Me to Feel Suicidal?

There are some medications that can cause a person to feel suicidal. This is a side effect typically associated with the antidepressant called selective serotonin reuptake inhibitors. People under the age of 25 are especially at risk. If you start to experience suicidal feelings after taking antidepressants you will need to contact your doctor as soon as possible. If you feel as if you are on the verge of suicide go to your nearest hospital.

Why Do Some People Have a Higher Risk of Suicide?

Research has found that people who identify as lesbian, gay, bisexual or transsexual (LGBTQ) men, and people who suffer from Asperger's syndrome are more likely to commit suicide.

LGBTQ

Research has found that people who identify as LGBTQ carry more risk of experiencing suicidal feelings and taking their own lives. There are many complex reasons for this and they have yet to be fully understood. However, LGBTQ people often suffer from mental health problems that are linked to:

- Transphobia, biphobia, or homophobia

- Bullying

- Discrimination

They can also experience hostility, negative reactions, and rejection from friends, family, employers, strangers and certain religious groups. This can negatively affect self esteem which leads them to further isolate themselves and attempt to hide their sexuality from those around them.

Men

Studies have shown that more men than women commit suicide but the reasons are unclear. However, men often:

- Feel as if they should keep their thoughts and feelings to themselves and get on with life.

- Choose methods of suicide that will ensure their death.

- Believe that they have to cope with life's problems alone.

- Worry that they will be seen as weak if they get help or talk about their feelings.

Asperger's Syndrome

A study conducted by researchers from Cambridge University in the United Kingdom concluded that adults who suffer from Asperger's syndrome are more likely to experience suicidal thoughts than the average person.

Aspergers syndrome is a form of autism, sufferers find it difficult to communicate, they do not function well socially and they have a problem with repetitive behavior. According to research Asperger's has been linked to depression. The study found that 66% of Asperger's patients had suicidal thoughts, 35% had attempted or planned suicide in their lifetime. The study discovered that suicidal ideation was more common in Asperger's patients with a history of depression. They were four times more likely to suffer from suicidal thoughts than Asperger's patients that didn't have a history of depression.

Chapter 2: How Can I Get Help For Suicidal Feelings

If you are experiencing continuous suicidal feelings you may feel as if there is no way out. However, there are plenty of support groups that will give you the help that you need.

Support Through Your Doctor

Going to see your doctor is a good place to start. It is normal to feel worried about talking to your doctor about suicidal feelings especially if you are already familiar with him. However, they are used to hearing about such issues. Your doctor can do one or more of the following:

- Refer you to mental health services
- Prescribe you with medication

- Refer you to a psychotherapist or a counselor

A Counselor or Psychiatrist

Speaking to a professional such as a psychotherapist or a counselor will help you to understand why you are feeling suicidal. They will give you coping strategies to help you to resolve them.

Medication

Although there is no specific drug to target suicidal thoughts, your doctor can prescribe you with medication to tackle the underlying issue which is often related to mental health. Medication might include mood stabilizers, antipsychotics, or antidepressants.

Crisis Service

A crisis service helps people to resolve mental health issues at short notice. The following services are available:

- A home treatment and crisis resolution team can support individuals in their homes during a mental health crisis.

- A community mental health team can provide home support whether you are in a crisis or not.

- A crisis house provides a safe haven where people can go and speak to someone when they are feeling suicidal.

- Local support services provide issue specific support, counselling, drop in sessions and day services.

Telephone Services

Many telephone services are available 24 hours a day. They provide support and information when you need it that is judgment free and confidential. Speaking to someone on the phone can also be useful if you are finding it hard to open up to the people around you, or if you are not comfortable speaking to a person face to face.

Peer Support

Peer support is when people who have had similar experiences get together and support each other by talking about what they are going through. They share tips, thoughts and advice on the most effective coping strategies. There is also peer support online, some people prefer this if they are not comfortable speaking over the phone or face to face.

Chapter 3: How Can I Cope When I Have No Access to Anyone

There are going to be times when you can't get on the phone, get online or go and visit someone and you have to deal with your feelings alone. This can be a scary experience; however, it is important to remember that what you are feeling will pass because nothing lasts forever.

There are strategies that you can implement right now to stop you from acting on your suicidal thoughts. People are different; therefore, it is important that you find the method that works best for you. Here are some practical tips to assist you when you are feeling suicidal.

Getting Through The First Five Minutes

According to the New England Journal of Medicine between one-third to 80 percent of suicide attempts are acts of impulsiveness. Out of those who made a lethal attempt to kill themselves, 24 percent did so less than five minutes after making the decision. As you have read, the desire to commit suicide is often caused by an immediate stressor such as a loss of employment or a break up. Out of the people who do attempt to take their life and fail even after the most lethal attempt such as shooting themselves in the head, 90 percent don't make a second attempt. This statistic is a reflection of the temporary nature of a suicidal crisis.

In 1978, a study was conducted on 515 people who were talked down from the Golden Gate Bridge. It was found that over 26 years later 94 percent of them were either still alive or they had died from natural causes. Several rare Golden Gate Bridge suicide attempt survivors remember that they immediately regretted their decision as soon as they had jumped. In 2003, The New Yorker covered the story of Kevin Hines, at the age of 18 he jumped off the bridge and survived. He said that as soon as he had taken the leap he realized that he had made a mistake. His first thought after jumping was "Why am I doing this? I don't want to die!"

This is why getting through the first five minutes of your decision to commit suicide is so important. There is a high possibility that once you perform the act, you are going to regret it and so the most sensible idea is not to do it at all.

Here are 100 ways to get through the first five minutes of feeling suicidal:

1. Do some laundry
2. Reorganize your bedroom
3. Go shopping
4. Clean your house
5. Make an online purchase
6. Do yoga or meditate
7. Learn some new words
8. Plant something in your garden
9. Make a present for a loved one
10. Volunteer your time
11. Take some pictures
12. Write a story
13. Make a list of things you are proud of
14. Make a list of the things that you like most about yourself

15. Go and visit your neighbour

16. Kiss someone 50 times

17. Play with your pet

18. Sunbath

19. Watch a good movie

20. Start planning your next vacation

21. Bake some cookies

22. Drink something very hot or very cold

23. Do a puzzle

24. Watch something on YouTube

25. Watch your favorite television show

26. Do some exercise

27. Floss your teeth

28. Paint or draw on your body

29. Suck some ice cubes

30. Look for your pulse

31. Change your clothes

32. Have a hot shower

33. Massage your shoulders

34. Give yourself a haircut

35. Play with something soft like play-doh

36. Listen to your favorite songs

37. Start searching for an online date

38. Read something

39. Take an online quiz

40. Do a suduko puzzle

41. Eat something you like

42. Cook a nice meal

43. Eat some chocolate

44. Take a walk

45. Go driving

46. Sit outside

47. Stargaze or cloud watch

48. Take a trip to the beach

49. Go swimming

50. Count your socks

51. Count your breathing

52. Watch something that makes you laugh

53. Play some music and dance

54. Jump up and down on your bed

55. Break something

56. Count how long you can hold your breath

57. Move your furniture around

58. Start learning a new language

59. Do some origami

60. Play an instrument

61. Send yourself some flowers

62. Play a video game

63. Do a jigsaw puzzle

64. Do a crossword puzzle

65. Write a letter to the president

66. Perform a random act of kindness

67. Pack some old clothes to give away

68. Make a financial donation to a non profit organization

69. Contact your local church and offer to volunteer your time

70. Write a letter to your ex partner but don't post it

71. Draw a picture

72. Make a phone call

73. Organize the files on your laptop

74. Start writing a journal

75. Do some coloring

76. Take a bike ride

77. Make a list of your goals

78. Polish your mirrors

79. Put some make-up on

80. Paint your nails

81. Make paper airplanes

82. Change all of your profile pictures

83. Walk up and down your stairs

84. Braid your hair

85. Go for a run

86. Look at some old photos

87. Cut pictures out of a magazine

88. Count matchsticks

89. Listen to your favorite music

90. Play with your younger siblings

91. Iron some clothes

92. Do some laundry

93. Fold your clothes

94. Call an old friend

95. Make a to do list

96. Make a shopping list

97. Draw a picture

98. Sow something

99. Do some cross stitching

100. Eat something sweet

Get Away From Danger Zones And Harmful Objects

Suicidal thoughts can become overwhelming when you are in a potentially dangerous situation or area. If you are near weapons, guns, standing on a balcony, driving, or waiting for a train, physically move away from the situation to reduce the risk of you acting on your suicidal thoughts. If you have any weapons or medications in your home ask a family member or a friend to remove them.

Take Deep Breaths

When breathing is slowed down it helps to slow the heart rate and supply oxygen to the brain. The process of slowing down your breathing will get you to focus on your breathing instead of the suicidal thoughts. Regain control of your breath by inhaling for four seconds and then exhaling for four seconds. Repeat this until you feel that your breathing has slowed down.

Using Your Senses

Close your eyes for a few seconds and then open them. Focus your gaze on whatever you are surrounded by. Regardless of what you are looking at, try and describe it in as much detail as possible. What can you hear? What do the walls look like? What does the ground look like? Imagine that you are writing a book and you need to be as detailed as possible. Use as many of your senses as you can to take your focus off the suicidal thoughts.

Muscle Relaxations

When you are feeling overwhelmed, your muscles tighten up without you being conscious of it. You may turn your hands into fists, clench your jaw or flex your shoulders.

Set your mind on relaxing your muscles, begin with your head and work your way down relaxing each muscle group as you go along. You can also give your neck and shoulders a massage to loosen up.

Reach Out

If the above techniques are not working, you are going to have to reach out to someone for help. This is often a last resort for people with suicidal tendencies because they don't like to feel as if they are a burden. However, if you are reading this I am assuming it's because you want to get better; therefore, you are going to have to do something extreme to keep yourself alive even if you don't want to.

Instead of isolating yourself and shutting down, surround yourself with people you know care about you and want to help you. If you really feel as if you don't have any friends and there isn't anyone you can trust call a helpline, they will be able to assist you in recovery.

When people are recovering from an illness such as cancer friends and family will typically come and visit them. The same help and support can assist you in recovering from suicidal thoughts.

Don't allow your fears and worries about being alone in your struggle prevent you from letting others know that you are having suicidal thoughts. As you have read, there are professional services that can assist in your recovery. A suicidal person is no different from any other person who is sick or has been injured; you need treatment to get better.

If you feel as if you are in an urgent situation, don't hesitate to call 911. Your first priority should be your safety and there are professionals available who can help you.

Remind Yourself That Recovery is Possible

You are not the first person who has suffered from suicidal thoughts and you won't be the last. Many people have overcome suicidal thoughts and so can you, it's not impossible. There are people who have attempted to take their lives several times and are alive today to tell their story because there is a way out and it is essential that you remember this.

Think About The Reasons You Do Have to Live

People commit suicide because they feel as if they have nothing to live for. However, if you were to sit and think about the reasons you have to live you will find at least one thing. What are you looking forward to? Do you have family members that will be heartbroken because of your death?

If you really can't think of anything make some plans for the future. What countries would you like to visit? Do you want to go back to school? Think about goals or dreams that can inspire you to hold on.

Treat Yourself Kindly

Speak to yourself as if you are talking to someone you really do care about and tell them all the reasons why they mean so much to you. Take a bath using your favorite soaps. Wrap yourself up in a comfortable blanket and watch a movie. These ideas might sound silly but it can be easy to forget about treating yourself every once in a while.

Chapter 4: Build Your Self Esteem

One of the underlying causes of suicide is low self esteem. When you don't value yourself and you feel hopeless and helpless you are going to feel as if you don't have anything to offer the world. As you know this is a dangerous place to be in because if you don't feel as if you can be of any benefit to the world, what's the point of being in it? This is where the foundation for suicide is laid. However, if you can find the strength to shift your frame of mind into believing that you are worth something and that you are valuable you will experience a radical transformation in your thought process. It is essential that you can build and maintain a high level of self esteem; here are some of the reasons why:

Life Becomes Lighter and Simpler

When you love and like yourself life gets easier. The paranoia will stop; you won't beat yourself up or drag yourself down over the smallest mistakes, or feel that there is something wrong with you because you haven't reached an impossible perfect inhuman standard.

You Will Be More Stable

When you value yourself you will stop trying to get attention and validation from other people. As you become less needy, you won't be on a constant emotional roller coaster as a result of what others say or think about you today or in two weeks time.

Less Self-Sabotage

There is no enemy worse than self. When you have high self-esteem, you will feel as if you deserve good things to happen in your life. You will be motivated to achieve your goals because you believe that you deserve them. You will stop self-sabotaging which is the main reason for failure.

You Will Become More Attractive in a Relationship

There is nothing worse than being in a relationship with a person who has low self esteem. Your partner won't feel the burden of having to lift you up every time you decide to have a moment of hysteria. You won't cause a massive scene if your boyfriend runs into one of female friends in the mall. Everyone wants a drama free relationship and only people with a high-self esteem can provide this.

Now that you know why you should improve your self esteem, let's look at the practical steps you can take to improving your self esteem.

Shut Down Your Inner Critic

We all have an inner critic that tells us we are hopeless, worthless and that we will never amount to anything in life. You can make the choice whether you want to listen to this voice or not. One way to shut this voice down is to say the word "Stop" whenever you hear it. You can also say something like, "I am not going to entertain these negative thoughts about myself." Once you have said what you need to say to yourself, refocus your thoughts on something more constructive.

Healthy Motivation Habits

To further silence your inner critic it helps to have habits that are going to motivate you. Here are some helpful tips:

- **Review the Benefits:** A simple but powerful motivational technique is to write down the benefits you will gain from achieving your goals. For example, if you want to lose weight, one of the benefits is that you will have more energy to do the things that you like. If your goal is to make more money, one of the benefits will be that you can travel more. When you have written out your list put it in a position where you will be able to see it and review it daily such as the bathroom mirror or the refrigerator.

- **Focus on Doing What You Enjoy:** When you enjoy doing something it is easy to find the motivation to do it. When you are passionate about achieving your goals, it is easier to penetrate the inner resistance that is so common when trying to reach a target. If you ever find yourself losing motivation ask yourself whether you are doing something that you are truly passionate about. If not, refocus and start working on what you know you will enjoy.

After using your stop word or phrase, incorporate one of the above techniques. After a while you will have developed a habit and your inner critic won't be so loud.

Take a Self Appreciation Break

This habit is fun and simple; if you spend 2 minutes each day doing this it will make a huge difference in your life.

Start by taking a deep breath and then ask yourself the following question: "What 3 things do I appreciate about myself?" Here are some example answers:

- I motivate and inspire people through what I write.
- I am determined to achieve my goals in life.
- I am grateful for the life I have.

They don't have to be big things, if they are big that's great, but three small things will do. A short appreciation break not only helps you to develop self esteem in the long run, it can also turn your bad mood into a good mood and revive your positive energy.

Do The Right Thing

Integrity is a must when it comes to building self esteem. Your behavior in front of people doesn't define your character, it's what you do behind closed doors when no one is looking that counts. Have you ever filed illegal tax returns? Did the casher give you an extra $20 change and you realized and kept it? All these things will determine whether or not you have integrity, when you can say with confidence that you are a man or a woman of integrity that is a big achievement because the majority of people in life are going to cut corners if they can get away with it.

Stop Trying to be a Perfectionist

There is no such thing as perfection and the more you attempt to strive for it the more disappointed you are going to become. Perfectionism is a very destructive habit; it can hold you back from doing what is required of you because you are scared of failing. This leads to procrastination which means you don't have the time you need to get the job done making it impossible to achieve the results that you want. This will then cause your self esteem to plummet even further. On the flip side of this you are quick to take action but you are never satisfied with what you have achieved which further erodes your self esteem.

Here are some techniques to overcome perfectionism:

- **Just be Good Enough:** When you realize that there is something called "good enough" it will take the pressure off you to over perform. This doesn't mean that you shouldn't put your best effort forward, do the best you can with "good enough" in mind.

- **Remember How Harmful Perfectionism Can be:** When you are a perfectionist you are not only harming yourself you are also harming others around you. Perfectionists typically place the same standards on everyone else that they do on themselves. This can make other people feel bad because you are constantly criticizing their performance. It is helpful to remember that life isn't a book, a song or a film, people make mistakes and you shouldn't expect the world to fit into your box.

Handle Failures and Mistakes In a Positive Way

Anytime you step outside of your comfort zone, or you attempt to accomplish anything of value you are going to run into some obstacles along the way. This is normal and this is alright, anyone who has ever achieved anything of substance in life failed first, in fact it was their failure that led to their success. Any time you are working on a project and it goes wrong, use it as an opportunity to do something even more spectacular. The next time you fail at something, do the following:

- **Become Your Own Best Friend:** Would your friends, parents and siblings support you if you made a mistake? Of course they would, and this is how you should treat yourself. Talk to yourself and encourage yourself the way they would, this will keep you from falling into a depression and help you to become more creative and constructive so that you can rectify the mistake.

- **Be Optimistic:** When you have made a mistake ask yourself what you can learn from it? What opportunity can you find in your failure? If you look hard enough and stop focusing on the negative you will find something positive that you can build upon.

Treat Other People With Kindness

I am a firm believer in karma, and if you treat people bad it will come right back to you. When you are kind to others, people in turn will be kind to you and this will boost your self esteem. Every day you should focus on being kind to others, here are some helpful tips:

- Listen to someone who wants to vent.

- Hold the door open for the person behind you.

- Allow someone to get in your lane when you are driving.

- Encourage a family member or friend when they are not feeling motivated.

- Take the time out of your day to help someone in a practical way.

Do Something You've Never Done Before

When you give yourself the challenge of trying something new it forces you to step outside of your comfort zone. Once you realize that you are capable of being successful at something other than what you are familiar with you will begin to value yourself. You may not have been the best at it but you were successful because you made the effort. This is something that you should appreciate about yourself. Make it a regular part of your life to do something out of the ordinary and your self esteem will grow tremendously.

Stop Comparing Yourself to Others

You are unique, special and extraordinary; there is no one on the face of the earth like you. It is important that you learn to see yourself like this or you will keep comparing yourself to others when they have their own unique qualities that are different from yours. Learn to appreciate yourself for who you are and become the best version of you instead of a cheap replica of someone else. There is nothing more appealing than an authentic person.

Comparing yourself to other people is a very destructive habit because you can never win. There is always going to be someone better looking, with more money or with a better job than you. If you are going to make judgments about yourself based on other people you are never going to be satisfied. Have you ever met a person who tries to outdo everyone? They are never satisfied with themselves and they are always trying to be number one. They might be at the top of their game career wise but because you've decided that you want to become a motivational speaker all of a sudden they want to do the same and become the best at it too. This is how you will end up if you don't stop comparing yourself to people.

Spend Time With Positive People

To be successful at this you are probably going to have to get rid of some friends. If you suffer from low self esteem, it's possible that your friends also suffer from low self-esteem and you sit around having pity parties together. This is going to have to stop, if you want to increase your level of confidence you are going to have to surround yourself with positive people who want the best out of life and who are going to support you on your journey to wholeness.

This also applies to what you read and listen to. Do you spend your TV time watching mindless soap operas or talk shows? I'm sure you have heard the phrase "Garbage in, garbage out." This basically means that whatever you allow in through your eyes and ears is what you will end up valuing. Start watching programs and reading books that will educate you and listen to things that will inspire and uplift you. You will soon start to notice a difference in how you view yourself.

Chapter 5: Why Do People Commit Suicide

Suicide is one of the leading causes of death worldwide. There has been a limited amount of research into the causes. The assumption is that the majority of people who kill themselves do so because they are depressed. This is true in some cases but not in all of them. According to psychological studies, here are some of the reasons why people take their own lives.

Vulnerable to Suicide

Experts believe that there are several things that determine how vulnerable an individual is to suicidal thoughts and behavior. These include:

Depression: The feelings experienced during a major depression are more than a heavy feeling of sadness. Cancer survivors who suffer from depression have described the depression as worse than the illness. They describe a blackness that envelopes them and pushes everything else out. The pain is so intense that it is almost physical and they have a desperate desire to escape the unbearable feeling. When depression leads to suicide it is accompanied by feelings of hopelessness.

Spite: A recent story in the United Kingdom described a woman who killed her child and then attempted to kill herself. Before she smothered her two year old daughter to death she sent a picture of her daughter to the child's father, her former partner who had recently ended the relationship. The text message read something along the lines of "I thought you deserved to see her one last time." Even though she was unsuccessful in killing herself, her main motive was to get back at the boyfriend who no longer wanted to be with her.

This suicide gesture is typically an attempt to manipulate others into getting what they want through the threat of suicide. This threat can often go further than it was intended and result in the death of the person. There are certain drugs that when taken alone can be harmless; however, when they are combined with other drugs they can be fatal and it is often this ignorance that causes accidental death.

Mental Illness: Psychological illnesses such as schizophrenia will cause people to have delusions that they are being persecuted so badly that they feel that suicide is their only escape.

These suicides often don't reflect a desire for death but a desperation to get out of the situation by doing something irrational such as shooting at a policeman or jumping out of a window.

Defiance: Teenagers and young adults will often kill themselves because of defiance. A psychiatrist described a story of a young man who refused to allow his parents to control him. He told them that he could take his own life if he wanted to and there was nothing they could do to stop him. They had him sectioned and restrained on a number of occasions. The last time he was released from hospital he took his life by throwing himself in front of a train.

Hatred: This is typically the motive behind people who kill a former lover and then take their own life. Or someone who is fired from a job, returns to his place of employment kills everyone and then kills himself. It is their last attempt to get even and they would rather die then face the consequences. There are some people who feel that their family have wronged them in some irredeemable way and the only way to get back at them is to let them live with the torment and guilt of finding them dead. They will kill themselves in a location where they know a family member will find them.

Loneliness: There are some people who will kill themselves because someone close to them has died such as a spouse or a parent. For people who believe that there is an afterlife death is their way of leaving earth to be with that person.

Self Hatred: The feeling of hatred for oneself, where an individual becomes so fed up with their inability to live up to the world's standards that they take their own life. There are some suicides that don't just reflect a desire to die but to be wiped off the face of the earth completely. Such as jumping off a building or jumping in front of a train.

Chagrin: An ordinary failure in life can lead some people to take their life. There have been stories of students committing suicide because they received a B grade instead of the A they are used to. The dreaded fear of failure is often the result of extremely strict parents who put unrealistically high expectations on their children. The lover who gets discarded by their partner is another example.

Helplessness: Hermann Goering took his life by drinking poison the day before his execution. It was his way of taking control of his life out of the hands of his executioners. Patients who have been told they only have a certain amount of time to live will often take their own lives.

Attention Seeking: People who feel insignificant in life will often kill themselves for fame or remembrance. Such individuals will choose a flamboyant way to die such as jumping off a theatre balcony in the middle of a performance.

Not all of the motives mentioned are going to be black and white, some of them will overlap. There are also going to be much more complicated explanations as to why a person decided to take their own life. There are some people who are going to have more than one reason as a motive for suicide.

None of the situations described are rational; but depending on your worldview, there is such a thing as rational suicide. When an individual is suffering from an incurable and painful illness the majority of people would understand why the sick person chose to take their life.

Chapter 6: Why Suicidal People Find it so Hard to Recover

Sexual assault survivors, combat veterans and other trauma victims typically suffer from a condition referred to as Post-Traumatic Stress Disorder (PTSD). The symptoms of the condition destabilizes a person so much that they are unable to live a normal life.

People who suffer from suicidal ideation or those who have attempted suicide may be victims of PTSD. According to the definition of the condition people become vulnerable to PTSD when they go through something that the majority of people don't experience. This could be a car accident, watching someone die, or being severely abused.

People who are suicidal have all the symptoms of a person who suffers from PTSD. The majority of people in a suicide crisis don't have a severe and prolonged crisis. The immediate feeling is that they are unable to cope with life and they are at breaking point at that instant. Since 30,000 people per year commit suicide in America alone, it is clear that this is a big problem.

Many suicidal people are haunted by memories of a former crises, periods when they were severely depressed or self-harming. Suicidal people suffer from PTSD simply because they were once suicidal and there have been a significant number of traumas that contributed to them becoming suicidal such as child sexual abuse or the death of a loved one, and it is important that they are addressed during recovery.

The PTSD research for sexual abuse survivors and veterans lists symptoms that are typical amongst survivors of such trauma. Each individual is different and so the symptoms and severity will differ from person to person. A large number of these symptoms are typical among people who have a long term history of suicidal ideation. These symptoms include the following.

Invasive Thoughts: Vivid, intrusive and persistent memories regarding the traumatic situation can cause deep distress. Daily life events can trigger upsetting memories relating to the trauma. They also suffer from memory loss regarding certain parts of the traumatic event. A lot of suicidal people are tormented by images such as the belief that their body has a bomb inside it, or that there is a knife hanging over their head. During recovery, they will often discover that these images have played an important role in their desire to commit suicide.

Fear: The fear that the traumatic event will happen again can lead suicidal people to isolate themselves. For example, if they were involved in a serious car accident, they develop a fear of getting into vehicles whether it's a car or public transportation. This then leads to them staying at home because it's impossible to get anywhere without using some form of transportation unless the distance is short enough to walk.

Self Blame: Sexual abuse survivors often blame themselves for their attack. The thought process is along the lines of: "If I hadn't gone to that club, if I hadn't been wearing such a short skirt. If only I hadn't got so drunk then it would never have happened." This thought process is also found in the loved ones of people who were successful in committing suicide. They will often think along the lines of: "If only I had got him some help when he said he was suicidal, if only I had taken her seriously." Such thoughts are often coping mechanisms in fear that there will be another suicide in the family; the idea is that if I handle things properly I can prevent it from happening again. It is more tolerable for surviving family members to imagine that they could have done more to stop it than to have feelings of total helplessness.

The Inability to Adjust to Normal Life: PTSD sufferers have stated that when they have attempted to get on with life they find it difficult to readjust to such things as employment, family and relationships. Veterans have reported that they feel as if they never came back from the war, that they are still there. People who were once suicidal have reported that they feel as if they are still stuck in that moment.

People who have experienced a traumatic event are often told that they should get on with their lives and forget about what happened in the past. Others wonder why they find it so difficult to enjoy life like a normal person. If it was that simple the term PTSD wouldn't exist. PTSD helps to explain why it is so difficult for people who suffer from suicidal ideation to recover. Due to the fact that a person has been suicidal they suffer from many of the symptoms that are associated with post-traumatic stress disorder. Outside of PTSD, these conditions are serious and they create almost impenetrable barriers during the recovery process.

Although it is difficult, healing is possible, suicidal people can heal from the original trauma that triggered suicidal ideation, and they can also heal from the PTSD symptoms that have haunted them since the trauma. Here are some steps to overcome PTSD:

Challenging Unwanted Thoughts

One of the symptoms of PTSD is negative thinking and it can have a profound effect on your mood. The majority of these harmful and negative thoughts take place outside of your control and it can be difficult to monitor them.

When you catch yourself thinking unwanted thoughts it's important to remember that they are only thoughts, they are not facts and they don't have any real basis. Although you might actually believe a lot of the negative thoughts when you have been through a traumatic event or when you are feeling stressed and low, it is important to remember that your thought process is based on wrong assumptions and you should challenge them.

If you are thinking about things in an unhelpful and unrealistic way, the following section will help you to identify when this is taking place. When you are capable of recognizing your thoughts you can learn how to look at things realistically which will improve your mood. Here are some examples of unhealthy negative thinking:

- I am unable to cope

- I am helpless

- Something is going to happen to me, I am in danger

- Everything is my fault

- The world is threatening and dangerous

When you start this process you are going to find it difficult to identify your negative thoughts. Instead, you might want to try thinking about a specific moment when your mood changed. Maybe you were thinking about a traumatic experience; think about what was going through your mind at that time.

Unhealthy Thought Patterns

Your first step is to recognize an unhealthy thought so that you can challenge it. When you are aware of the typical patterns that lead to negative thinking you will find it easier to recognize them. Here are some of the typical patterns that lead to negative thinking:

- **Worry:** When people are anxious or worried about something it is normal for them to over think the situation. This leads to an overactive imagination as you start to picture what could go wrong. Instead of just leaving the situation alone, you completely exaggerate the event and convince yourself that a major catastrophe is going to take place.

- **Sensitivity:** Emotionally vulnerable people are very sensitive, and anything that is said that they consider out of context is taken to heart. For example:

  - You are worried about taking an exam and a friend is having a conversation about how someone failed the same subject. You automatically assume that they are implying that you are going to fail too.

- **Focused on the Negative:** PTSD sufferers find it difficult to acknowledge the positive aspects of their life. The only things they think they are capable of seeing are negative. This way of thinking prevents you from feeling good about yourself and causes you to have low self esteem.

- **No Grey Area:** When people are only capable of seeing things in black or white, without an in between or a grey area it causes them to have a polarized view of the world. This can lead to setting unattainable high standards, a failure to recognize achievement as well as being overly critical.

- **No Hope For The Future:** As a result of one isolated incident you are led to assume that everything else is going to follow the same pattern. You find it difficult to see a negative event as something that just happened once. This can lead to you attaching negative labels to yourself which affects your confidence and your mood, which then lead to feelings of hopelessness.

There are several techniques you can learn to help you to challenge your negative thoughts which will improve your mood.

Challenging Negative Thinking

Once you have recognized the negative thought ask yourself the following questions:

- What evidence is there that can contradict this negative thought?

- What patterns of negative thinking can you identify?

- What would you say to a friend or a family member who was thinking like you?

- Are there any benefits associated with the way you are thinking?

- How will you feel six months down the line about the way you are thinking?

- Is there any other way you can look at the situation?

When you are answering your questions write the answers down so that you can go back over them once you are done. You can then try and come up with a more rational and balanced view to your thinking.

Relaxation

It's important to take the time out to unwind and relax by participating in activities that you enjoy. This can help to elevate your mood by calming your mind and body; it can also help you to get a good night's sleep. Without taking time out to relax, it's easy to feel stressed out and overwhelmed by life.

Relaxation can take the form of participating in an activity or you can simply spend some time alone. Some good examples include taking a hot bath or reading a book. Exercise is also a good way of relaxing because it causes the body to release endorphins which are also referred to as the feel good hormone. What you do isn't important, what's important is that do something that you are going to look forward to and gives you relief from your normal activities. When you are taking part in an activity that you enjoy, you will spend less time worrying. Here is a list of some relaxing activities:

- Visit a family member or a friend

- Go and see a movie

- Go to a concert

- Take a road trip

- Go on vacation

These are just suggestions, you can also make a list of ideas that you might enjoy.

Try and find the time to relax on a daily basis, you don't have to do something like go to the movie theatre, but reading a book, or taking a hot bath is something that you can incorporate into your daily routine.

Controlled Breathing

This is a very relaxing exercise, it is simple but effective and involves focusing on your breathing and slowing it down. This can be particularly helpful for people who feel light headed or dizzy when they feel stressed or worried. When people are distressed their breathing accelerates which can limit the flow of oxygen to the brain. This can be an unpleasant and uncomfortable experience which makes a person feel even more anxious which then triggers a vicious cycle. Learning how to control your breathing can help you to effectively manage these feelings. It also gives your body and mind the opportunity to calm down.

You can use this exercise at any time to help you to relax when you are feeling anxious. You can also use it to help you sleep.

- Get yourself into a comfortable position
- Breathe in for four seconds
- Hold the breath for two seconds

- Breathe out for four seconds

Repeat this for a few minutes until you start to feel relaxed, if you were feeling dizzy you should also start to feel it lift.

Limit Avoidance

The easiest way to get over your fears is to confront them. When you get into the habit of avoiding situations you will make the problem even worse. The more time you spend avoiding a situation the more intimidating it will become. When you avoid a situation you also prevent yourself from proving that you are capable of coping with it. As a result, your anxiety will continue and your confidence will remain low.

When you confront the situation that you are afraid of, your confidence will increase and your anxiety will improve. When the body reacts to stress, anxiety or fear it is referred to as the fight or flight response and it prepares the body to take action. We either escape from the danger or we protect ourselves against it. Here is what happens to your body during the fight or flight response:

- The heart beats faster to supply the muscles with more blood

- You produce more sweat so that the body can cool itself down

- You tense your muscles to get them ready for action

- You take quicker and deeper breaths to supply oxygen to the muscles

- Bodily functions such as digestion that are not needed are shut down

- Quick thinking to narrow down the best option to survive

This reaction is always going to be of benefit to us, historically it was even more of an advantage because we were hunters and gatherers. The fight or flight response protected us against predators. Today we do not need to depend so much on fighting or running to negotiate difficult circumstances which means that the symptoms described are not as helpful. Potential threats such as walking alone in the dark, hearing a loud noise, or someone walking closely behind you does not need such extreme physical reactions. If you feel like this constantly it is likely that your body is in a state of high alert which can be dangerous in the long run. The fight or flight response releases cortisone into the blood stream which is also known as the stress hormone. It is beneficial when released for a short period of time because it lets the body know that it needs to protect itself. However, when it is constantly in the blood stream it can cause a number of conditions such as:

- Weight gain

- Concentration and memory impairment

- Sleep problems

- Heart disease

- Headaches

- Digestive problems

- Depression

- Anxiety

It is important that you recognize these feelings in your body. This will let you know when you are getting anxious or worrying too much, you can then take the necessary steps to eliminate the feelings through breathing exercises or relaxation. When you are exposed to the situation that you are afraid of and you deal with the anxiety, over time your fear of the situation will diminish.

Socialize

When you experience a traumatic event your motivation to live life is going to decrease. You may find that you stop participating in activities or hobbies that you were once passionate about. As time goes on you can end up not doing very much at all. This will lead to you feeling even more depressed.

Planning your week will motivate you to do more; this activity really assists in elevating your mood because it provides you with a visual of activities of things that you are looking forward to. Here is some advice on how to plan your week.

Filling Out Your Diary

When you are planning your week, start by writing down all the essential activities such as going to work, going food shopping, attending meetings or appointments and doing the housework. This will let you know what free time you have available so that you can start planning other activities that you will enjoy. Here are some ideas of things that you can schedule in your diary:

- **Socializing with friends and family**: Although you may not feel like it, social contact will make you feel better.

- **Hobbies and Interests:** These are activities that you might have enjoyed prior to the tragic event taking place. Or you might want to start working on a new project.

- **Exercise:** Endorphins are referred to as the feel good hormone and so exercising can improve your mood.

- **Alone Time:** Find the time to relax and to give yourself some space between your activities.

After filling out your diary, your next step is to try and follow through on the plan every day. Don't worry if things come up that you didn't anticipate, that's perfectly normal, in fact it's highly unlikely that you will be able to follow your plan to the letter. It's also ok if you want to be flexible and change some activities around. If you don't have the time for certain things just leave them out. Try and relax if you have to make changes.

A Support Group

Getting into a support group is very beneficial because you will have the opportunity to discuss your history of suicide with other people who understand and without the fear that you will be sectioned for doing so. You can talk about:

- Your crippling sense of personal weakness

- The contempt and hatred that you have for yourself and the rest of the world for not understanding

- Acts of self harm

- The confusion

- The pain

- The fears

- The isolation

In a support group you will learn that you are not alone and that there are indeed many people like you who are going through exactly the same experience. You won't have the severity of your condition minimized, belittled or denied. Over time your pain will decrease and those debilitating symptoms of PTSD will disintegrate.

Chapter 7: What to Look For in a Suicidal Person

It can be difficult to identify suicidal thoughts in family, friends and loved ones. The majority of people who have a desire to commit suicide are not open about how they are feeling. However, they will often leave clues. These are some of the warning signs that someone you know is at risk of suicide.

Discussing Suicide

Often when a person starts talking about harming themselves it's a cry for help. If you hear someone you know mention that they want to take their life get them help immediately. If the individual has started to withdraw from friends and family, they may feel helpless and trapped. Make sure that you don't leave this person alone and let them know that you are going to get help. The National Suicide Prevention Lifeline states that you should call 1-800-273-TALK to get in contact with a crisis center.

Depression or Bipolar Disorder

The overwhelming feelings associated with depression or bipolar disorder can lead people to contemplate suicide. The Director for the American Foundation for Suicide Prevention Paula Clayton states that depression is the leading cause of suicide, so the worse the depression gets, the more hopeless and helpless they feel.

Bipolar disorder is a condition where a person goes through periods of extreme happiness and extreme sadness. Suicide risk is higher during times of sadness.

Things to Listen For

- There isn't any point in me being alive

- Everyone would be better off if I wasn't here

- Next time I will make sure I take enough pills to get the job done properly

- I don't need these things anymore you can have them

- Don't worry, I'm not going to be here to deal with that

- When I'm gone you are going to be sorry

- Life is too difficult, I can't handle it

- I won't have to burden you for much longer

- I am so misunderstood

- There is nothing I can do to make things right

- I would be better off dead

- I can't see any way out of this

- You would be better off if I wasn't here

You may have noticed them doing some of the following activities:

- Getting things in order, paying their debts and changing their will

- Giving away things of value

- Writing a suicide note

- The purchase of a weapon

Chapter 8: How to Handle a Call From a Suicidal Person

You might have picked up this book because you know someone who has suicidal tendencies and you are unsure of how to react when they call you when they are having a crisis. Here are some tips to assist you.

- **Be Yourself:** There is no need to start acting like a doctor or trying to come up with medical terminology to get them to calm down, just be yourself. You don't have to have the right words, if you are truly concerned the other person will be able to hear it in your voice.

- **Listen:** Sometimes when a person is in a crisis, the best thing you can do is listen.

The more they are able to speak about how they are feeling the better position you will both be in. It gives the person the opportunity to release the hurt and gives you insight into what they are actually going through.

- **Be Sympathetic:** Your manner should be calm, patient, accepting and non-judgemental because the caller has taken a very important step in getting the help they need to deal with their suicidal thoughts.

- **Ask the Question:** The person might not call and tell you that they are having suicidal thoughts but they are saying things like "I can't live like this anymore, I'm so depressed." At this point you will need to ask "Are you having suicidal thoughts?" By asking this question you are letting him know that he can trust you to share his thoughts with you.

- **If the Answer is Yes:** If the person on the phone says that they are having suicidal thoughts you will need to start asking more questions such as:

  - Are you thinking about how you are going to carry the suicide out? (PLAN)

  - Do you have what you need to do it? (MEANS)

  - Are you thinking about when you are going to take action? (TIME SET) Approximately 95 percent of all suicidal people will answer no to some of these questions or state that they

are planning on killing themselves
sometime in the near future. This is a
good thing.

- **Let Them Talk:** When a suicidal person
is given the opportunity to talk about their
problems it will give them relief from pent
up feelings, loneliness, the feeling that
they are misunderstood and the comfort
that someone else cares enough to listen.
After speaking for a long period of time,
they will get tired which will alter the
chemistry in their body enabling them to
get a good night's sleep.

- **Avoid Arguments:** Don't try and sort
their problems out, all a suicidal person
needs is a shoulder to cry on. What might
sound like nothing to you is massive to

them and when you start giving your opinion it can turn into an argument. Unless they specifically ask you for advice keep it to yourself. The problem isn't the issue; the issue is how badly the person is hurting because of the problem.

- **Get The Details:** If the caller has taken drugs find out what they are, how much they have taken, when their last meal was, and their general health. At the same time as getting this information you should call the ambulance. This may be just a cry for help but it can also be fatal if they have taken the right combination of drugs.

Chapter 9: How Can I Help a Suicidal Person?

Take Them Seriously

Just because a person is talking about suicide doesn't mean that they aren't going to do it. Yes it's true that the majority of people who suffer from suicidal ideation don't go through with it. However, we don't know who is going to take their life and who isn't. Anyone who expresses the need to take their life requires immediate attention.

While it is true that the majority of people who kill themselves have been diagnosed with a mental illness this is not the case for everyone. Don't assume that because your friend doesn't suffer from bipolar they can't commit suicide.

Remember that everyone is different, while you may get over being jilted by your lover in a week, someone else might feel as if they can't live without the person and decide to take their own life. You have to pay attention

It's a Cry For Help

There is a myth that once a person decides to take their life there is nothing that can be done about it. The fact that the individual has made someone aware of how they feel and that they are still alive is evidence that they want help. They may have a deep desire to die but there is something inside them that has a desire to live and it is this part that is making the phone call. If a suicidal person reaches out to you it is because they believe that you care and that you can help them, they trust you.

Be Willing to Get Help Immediately

Preventing suicide isn't something that you do at the last minute. When you get a phone call make sure that you get help immediately. Suicidal people have a tendency to believe that trying to get help is going to cause them more anguish. That they are going to be judged for how they are feeling. You should take every necessary step to make sure that you get help for the suicidal person to limit instead of intensify their pain.

Don't Leave Them Alone

If you can get to the person's home do so, get rid of anything that they could use to harm themselves. This may include weapons, medication, alcohol, sheets and ropes. If you have to call an ambulance do so, but make sure that you don't leave them alone.

Don't Promise Confidentiality

A suicidal person might instruct you not to tell anyone about what they have discussed with you. It is important that you let them know that you will be reporting them to health care professionals for their own safety. A life is at stake and if you don't do something about it someone could die.

Suicide Risk Levels

There are levels of risk when it comes to suicide and it is important that you are familiar with them:

Low: Having suicidal thoughts without a plan. The individual has stated that they won't commit suicide.

Moderate: Having suicidal thoughts. They have a plan but it isn't lethal, they mention that they won't commit suicide.

High: Having suicidal thoughts with a specific plan that is very lethal but they say they won't commit suicide.

Severe: Having suicidal thoughts, they have a plan that is lethal and specific. They have stated that they will commit suicide.

If the individual you are dealing with is in the high or severe level you will need to get them immediate help. A person at low or moderate risk level may just need someone to talk to at that moment.

It is a very courageous act to help someone in a suicide crisis; however it is also emotionally draining. You are dealing with a person who is possibly chronically depressed and by them unloading their emotions on you it could have an adverse effect on your mood. Don't allow it to affect you and make sure that you remain optimistic.

Conclusion

The fact that you have got to the end of this book is an indication that you have a strong desire to live. Before I leave I want to remind you that you are special and extraordinary, you are unique and authentic, there is no one on the earth that has been fashioned and designed like you. The fact that you are still alive means that there is still hope for you. There is an assignment on the earth for you; lives that you can change with your story, souls that you can ignite with your fire and zeal to live so don't give up!

- Suicidal feelings originate from problems that you can resolve.

- Although it may not feel like it when you are in a crisis, suicide is NOT the only option that you have.

- Your situation will get better, it may not happen overnight but no situation is ever permanent.

If you think that you might try and harm yourself or attempt to take your life, get help immediately and call your local emergency services number. There are trained professionals available who will be able to give you the help that you need.

Weeping is for a season, if you hold on eventually your tears will turn into joy!

Other books available by D.C. Johnson on Kindle, paperback and audio:

Are You In A Toxic Relationship? How to Let Go and Move On With Your Life

Cognitive Behavioral Therapy: Learn How To Use CBT And The Power Of The Mind To Overcome Negative Thinking, Addiction, Depression, Phobias, Anxiety And Panic Disorders

The Warrior Mindset: The Secrets of Learning How to Be Assertive And Go From Victimhood to Warriorhood

www.ingramcontent.com/pod-product-compliance
Lightning Source LLC
Chambersburg PA
CBHW031135250726
48655CB00002B/682